BARACK OBAMA
(b. 1961)

QUOTATIONS

OF

Barack Obama

APPLEWOOD BOOKS

ISBN 978-1-4290-9711-6

Manufactured in the USA

Barack Obama

BARACK HUSSEIN OBAMA II was born on August 4, 1961 in Honolulu, Hawaii, the only president born outside of the contiguous 48 States. Obama's mother, Ann Dunham, was an American from Wichita, Kansas, while his father, Barack Obama Sr., grew up in Kenya.

After graduating from high school in 1979, Obama attended Occidental College in Los Angeles, then transferred to Columbia University in New York, where he double-majored in political science and English literature. He graduated with a bachelor of arts degree in 1983. He enrolled at Harvard Law School in the fall of 1988 and graduated with a juris doctor *magna cum laude* in 1991. After accepting a position as Visiting Law and Government Fellow at the University of Chicago Law School, he taught constitutional law for twelve years.

Obama was elected to the Illinois Senate in 1996 and was reelected in 1998 and 2002. He formally announced his candidacy for the US Senate in January 2003 and won the general election in November 2004. As a United States senator he held various assignments on the Senate Committees for Foreign Relations, Environment and Public Works, and Veterans'

Affairs, as well as with Homeland Security and Governmental Affairs.

On February 10, 2007, Obama announced his candidacy for president of the United States. He campaigned on ending the Iraq War, increasing energy independence, and reforming the United States healthcare system. He won the presidential election of 2008, making him the United States' first African American president. Running for reelection in 2012, he won 332 electoral votes and became the first Democratic president since Franklin Roosevelt to win the majority of the popular vote twice.

During his presidency Obama made good on some of his campaign promises, specifically the Affordable Care Act and the Paris climate change agreement. As a Democratic president dealing with a Republican-led Congress, he faced a political atmosphere during his presidency that was often contentious and hostile. Since leaving office he has remained active in Democratic politics, including campaigning for candidates in various elections. He and his wife, Michelle LaVaughn Robinson Obama, have been married since 1992 and have two daughters, Malia and Sasha.

QUOTATIONS
OF
Barack Obama

*T*onight, we gather to affirm the greatness of our nation—not because of the height of our skyscrapers, or the power of our military, or the size of our economy. Our pride is based on a very simple premise, summed up in a declaration made over two hundred years ago: "We hold these truths to be self-evident, that all men are created equal, that they are endowed by their Creator with certain inalienable rights, that among these are life, liberty and the pursuit of happiness." That is the true genius of America—a faith in simple dreams, an insistence on small miracles.

—Speech at the Democratic National Convention, July 27, 2004

*T*here is not a liberal America and a conservative America—there is the United States of America. There is not a Black America and a White America and Latino America and Asian America— there's the United States of America.

—Speech at the Democratic National Convention, July 27, 2004

*F*ocusing your life solely on making a buck shows a certain poverty of ambition. It asks too little of yourself.... Because it's only when you hitch your wagon to something larger than yourself that you realize your true potential.

—Knox College commencement address, June 4, 2005

I am a prisoner of my own biography:
I can't help but view the American
experience through the lens of a black man
of mixed heritage, forever mindful of how
generations of people who looked like me
were subjugated and stigmatized, and the
subtle and not so subtle ways that race
and class continue to shape our lives.

—*The Audacity of Hope: Thoughts on Reclaiming
the American Dream* (2006)

I love America too much, am too invested
in what this country has become, too
committed to its institutions, its beauty, and
even its ugliness, to focus entirely on the
circumstances of its birth. But neither can I
brush aside the magnitude of the injustice
done, or erase the ghosts of generations
past, or ignore the open wound, the
aching spirit, that ails this country still.

—*The Audacity of Hope: Thoughts on Reclaiming
the American Dream* (2006)

$\mathcal{E}$mpathy is a quality of character that can change the world—one that makes you understand that your obligations to others extend beyond people who look like you and act like you and live in your neighborhood.

—Commencement address at the University of
Massachusetts Boston, June 2, 2006

$\mathcal{I}$ recognize there is a certain presumptuousness in this, a certain audacity, to this announcement. I know that I haven't spent a lot of time learning the ways of Washington, but I've been there long enough to know that the ways of Washington must change. People who love their country can change it.

—Announcement of candidacy for President of
the United States, February 10, 2007

*C*hange will not come if we wait for some other person or if we wait for some other time. We are the ones we've been waiting for. We are the change that we seek.

—Speech to supporters, February 5, 2008

I know my country has not perfected itself. At times, we've struggled to keep the promise of liberty and equality for all of our people. We've made our share of mistakes, and there are times when our actions around the world have not lived up to our best intentions. But I also know how much I love America. I know that for more than two centuries, we have strived—at great cost and great sacrifice— to form a more perfect union; to seek, with other nations, a more hopeful world.

—Speech in Berlin, Germany, July 24, 2008

*M*any of you know that I got my name, Barack, from my father. What you may not know is that Barack is actually Swahili for "That One." And I got my middle name from somebody who obviously didn't think I'd ever run for president.

—Alfred E. Smith Memorial Foundation Dinner, October 16, 2008

*T*his victory alone is not the change we seek. It is only the chance for us to make that change. And that cannot happen if we go back to the way things were. It can't happen without you, without a new spirit of service, a new spirit of sacrifice. So let us summon a new spirit of patriotism, of responsibility, where each of us resolves to pitch in and work harder and look after not only ourselves but each other.

—Presidential election victory speech, November 4, 2008

*T*oday I say to you that the challenges we face are real. They are serious and they are many. They will not be met easily or in a short span of time. But know this, America— they will be met. On this day, we gather because we have chosen hope over fear, unity of purpose over conflict and discord. On this day, we come to proclaim an end to the petty grievances and false promises, the recriminations and worn-out dogmas, that for far too long have strangled our politics.

—First Inaugural Address, January 20, 2009

*W*ith hope and virtue, let us brave once more the icy currents, and endure what storms may come. Let it be said by our children's children that when we were tested we refused to let this journey end, that we did not turn back nor did we falter; and with eyes fixed on the horizon and God's grace upon us, we carried forth that great gift of freedom and delivered it safely to future generations.

—First Inaugural Address, January 20, 2009

*D*on't shortchange the future because of fear in the present.

—Press conference, April 1, 2009

*M*y administration has a job to do
as well. That job is to get this economy
back on its feet. That's my job, and it's
a job I gladly accept. I love these folks
who helped get us in this mess and then
suddenly say, "Well this is Obama's
economy." That's fine. *Give it to me.* My
job is to solve problems, not to stand on
the sidelines and carp and gripe. So, I
welcome the job. I want the responsibility.

—Remarks in Warren, Michigan, July 14, 2009

*W*e do not have to think that human nature is perfect for us to still believe that the human condition can be perfected. We do not have to live in an idealized world to still reach for those ideals that will make it a better place. The nonviolence practiced by men like Gandhi and King may not have been practical or possible in every circumstance, but the love that they preached—their fundamental faith in human progress—that must always be the North Star that guides us on our journey.

—Nobel Prize acceptance speech,
Oslo, Norway, December 9, 2009

*E*ach country will pursue a path rooted in the culture of its own people. Yet experience shows us that history is on the side of liberty, that the strongest foundation for human progress lies in open economies, open societies, and open governments. To put it simply, democracy, more than any other form of government, delivers for our citizens.

—Remarks to the United Nations General Assembly,
New York City, September 23, 2010

*B*ut at a time when our discourse has become so sharply polarized—at a time when we are far too eager to lay the blame for all that ails the world at the feet of those who think differently than we do—it's important for us to pause for a moment and make sure that we are talking with each other in a way that heals, not a way that wounds.

—Memorial service for the victims of the shooting
in Tucson, Arizona, January 12, 2011

*T*he presidency has a funny way of making a person feel the need to pray.

—National Prayer Breakfast, February 3, 2011

I know that people think I'm not passionate enough. That I'm too cool. That I'm too detached. But as I was going through my daily routine—sitting alone in my study, meditating, thinking about how to win the future—I pondered this critique, and calmly rejected it as thoroughly illogical. And for all those who think I golf too much, let me be clear. I'm not spending time on the golf course—I'm investing time on the golf course.

—Remarks at the Annual Gridiron Dinner, March 12, 2011

*N*othing comes to my desk that is perfectly solvable. Otherwise, someone else would have solved it. So you wind up dealing with probabilities. Any given decision you make, you'll wind up with a 30-to-40 percent chance that it isn't going to work. You have to own that and feel comfortable with the way you made the decision. You can't be paralyzed by the fact that it might not work out.

—*Vanity Fair*, October 2012

*W*e are not as divided as our politics suggests. We're not as cynical as the pundits believe. We are greater than the sum of our individual ambitions, and we remain more than a collection of red states and blue states.

—Re-election speech, Chicago, Illinois, November 6, 2012

*Y*ou and I, as citizens, have the power to set
this country's course. You and I, as citizens,
have the obligation to shape the debates of
our time—not only with the votes we cast,
but with the voices we lift in defense of our
most ancient values and enduring ideals.

—Second Inaugural Address, January 21, 2013

*T*hese days, I look in the mirror and
I have to admit, I'm not the strapping
young Muslim socialist that I used to be.

—White House Correspondents' Dinner, April 26, 2013

*T*rayvon Martin could have been me thirty-five years ago....There are very few African-American men in this country who haven't had the experience of being followed when they are shopping at a department store. That includes me. There are very few African American men in this country who haven't had the experience of walking across the street and hearing the locks click on the doors of cars.

—Remarks regarding the shooting of
Trayvon Martin, July 19, 2013

*W*e share a belief in the dignity and equality of every human being; that our daughters deserve the same opportunities as our sons; that our gay and lesbian brothers and sisters must be treated equally under the law; that our societies are strengthened and not weakened by diversity. And we stand up for universal human rights... because we believe that when these rights are respected, nations are more successful and our world is safer and more just.

—News conference with Prime Minister Reinfeldt
of Sweden, September 4, 2013

$\mathcal{N}$elson Mandela taught us the power of action, but he also taught us the power of ideas; the importance of reason and arguments; the need to study not only those who you agree with, but also those who you don't agree with. He understood that ideas cannot be contained by prison walls or extinguished by a sniper's bullet....

He demonstrated that action and ideas are not enough. No matter how right, they must be chiseled into law and institutions.

—Remarks at memorial service for former South African President Nelson Mandela, December 10, 2013

*S*o this is what America is prepared to do:
Taking action against immediate threats,
while pursuing a world in which the need
for such action is diminished. The United
States will never shy away from defending
our interests, but we will also not shy away
from the promise of this institution and its
Universal Declaration of Human Rights—the
notion that peace is not merely the absence
of war, but the presence of a better life.

—Address to the United Nations, September 24, 2014

*W*e need to reject any politics that targets
people because of race or religion. This isn't
a matter of political correctness. It's a matter
of understanding what makes us strong. The
world respects us not just for our arsenal;
it respects us for our diversity and our
openness and the way we respect every faith.

—Seventh State of the Union Address, January 12, 2016

*W*hatever you may believe, whether
you prefer one party or no party,
whether you supported my agenda or
fought as hard as you could against
it, our collective future depends on
your willingness to uphold your duties
as a citizen; to vote, to speak out, to
stand up for others—especially the weak,
especially the vulnerable—knowing
that each of us is only here because
somebody somewhere stood up for us.

—Seventh State of the Union Address, January 12, 2016

*W*e belong on the cutting edge
of innovation. That's an idea as old
as America itself. We're a nation
of tinkerers, and dreamers, and
believers in a better tomorrow.

—Remarks at White House Science Fair, April 12, 2016

*T*he America I know is full of courage, optimism, and ingenuity. The America I know is decent and generous.

—Remarks at the Democratic National Convention, July 28, 2016

*T*errorists will never be able to defeat the United States. Their only hope is to terrorize us into changing who we are or our way of life. That's why we Americans will never give in to fear. And it's why this weekend we remember the true spirit of 9/11. We're still the America of heroes who ran into harm's way; of ordinary folks who took down the hijackers; of families who turned their pain into hope. We are still the America that looks out for one another, bound by our shared belief that I am my brother's keeper, I am my sister's keeper.

—Weekly address, September 9, 2016

*M*y name may not be on the ballot, but
our progress is on the ballot. Tolerance is
on the ballot. Democracy is on the ballot.
Justice is on the ballot. Good schools are
on the ballot. Ending mass incarceration—
that's on the ballot right now.

—Remarks at the Congressional Black Caucus
Foundation Dinner, September 18, 2016

*A*nd in my own life, in this country,
and as president, I have learned that our
identities do not have to be defined by
putting someone else down, but can be
enhanced by lifting somebody else up. They
don't have to be defined in opposition
to others, but rather by a belief in liberty
and equality and justice and fairness.

—United Nations Address, September 20, 2016

*I*t is important to remember that capitalism
has been the greatest driver of prosperity
and opportunity the world has ever seen.

—*The Economist*, October 6, 2016

*T*hank you for everything. My last
ask is the same as my first. I'm asking
you to believe—not in my ability
to create change, but in yours.

—Twitter, following his Farewell Address,
January 10, 2017

*N*o one is born hating another person because of the color of his skin or his background or his religion...People must learn to hate, and if they can learn to hate, they can be taught to love...For love comes more naturally to the human heart than its opposite.

—Twitter, August 13, 2017

*T*he free press is under attack. Censorship and state control of media [are] on the rise. Social media—once seen as a mechanism to promote knowledge and understanding and solidarity—has proved to be just as effective promoting hatred and paranoia and propaganda and conspiracy theories.

—Nelson Mandela Annual Lecture, Johannesburg, South Africa, July 17, 2018

*A*ppealing to tribe, appealing to fear,
pitting one group against another, telling
people that order and security [would]
be restored if it weren't for those who
don't look like us or don't sound like us
or don't pray like we do—that's an old
playbook. It's as old as time. And in a
healthy democracy it doesn't work.

—Speech at the University of Illinois, September 7, 2018

*W*hen words stop meaning anything,
when truth doesn't matter, when people can
just lie with abandon, democracy can't work.

—Speech at a political rally, November 2, 2018

*T*his idea of purity and that you're never compromised and you're always politically woke—you should get over that quickly.... The world is messy. There are ambiguities. People who do really good stuff have flaws.

—Comments at an Obama Foundation event,
Chicago, October 29, 2019

*W*hat I can say for certain is that I'm not yet ready to abandon the possibility of America—not just for the sake of future generations of Americans but for all of humankind.

—From *A Promised Land* by Barack Obama (2022)

*T*he truth is, I've never been a big believer
in destiny. I worry that it encourages
resignation in the down-and-out and
complacency among the powerful. I
suspect that God's plan, whatever it
is, works on a scale too large to admit
our mortal tribulations; that in a single
lifetime, accidents and happenstance
determine more than we care to admit;
and that the best we can do is to try to
align ourselves with what we feel is right
and construct some meaning out of our
confusion, and with grace and nerve play
at each moment the hand that we're dealt.

—From *A Promised Land* by Barack Obama (2022)